Animals in Danger

in Europe

Louise and Richard Spilsbury

Raintree is an imprint of Capstone Global Library Limited, a company incorporated in England and Wales having its registered office at 7 Pilgrim Street, London, EC4V 6LB – Registered company number: 6695582

www.raintreepublishers.co.uk
myorders@raintreepublishers.co.uk

Text © Capstone Global Library Limited 2013
First published in hardback in 2013
Paperback edition first published in 2014
The moral rights of the proprietor have been asserted.

Edited by Rebecca Rissman, Dan Nunn, and Adrian Vigliano
Designed by Philippa Jenkins
Picture research by Tracy Cummins
Originated by Capstone Global Library Ltd
Printed in China by South China Printing Company Ltd

ISBN 978 1 406 26208 7 (hardback)
17 16 15 14 13
10 9 8 7 6 5 4 3 2 1

ISBN 978 1 406 26215 5 (paperback)
18 17 16 15 14
10 9 8 7 6 5 4 3 2 1

British Library Cataloguing in Publication Data
A full catalogue record for this book is available from the British Library.

Acknowledgements
We would like to thank the following for permission to reproduce photographs: Alamy pp. 17, 19 (© blickwinkel), 21 (© Chris Gomersall); Filipe Lopes p. 13 (© Filipe Lopes); Getty Images p. 29 (Catherine Ledner); istockphoto p. 11 (© Merlin Farwell); National Geographic Stock p. 26 (Joel Sartore); Nature Picture Library p. 27 (© Igor Shpilenok); NHPA pp. 22 (Hellio & Van Ingen), 25 (Dhritiman Mukherjee); Shutterstock pp. 4 (© Chris P.), 5 bottom (© Aleksander Bolbot), 5 top (© dimitris_k), 6 (© Christian Musat), 15 (© Rafa Irusta), 23 (©Peter Leahy), 28 (© Roca), icons (© Florian Augustin), (© tristan tan), maps (© AridOcean); Superstock pp. 9, 10, 14 (© NHPA), 18 (© Minden Pictures).

Cover photograph alpine ibex produced with permission of Shutterstock (© Peter Wey).
Cover photograph of a European bison reproduced with permission of Shutterstock (© MilousSK).
Cover photograph of a bluefin tuna reproduced with permission of Shutterstock (© holbox).
Cover photograph of a bluefin tuna in net reproduced with permission of istockphoto (© Gary Stokes).
Cover photograph of a Spanish lynx reproduced with permission of Superstock (© Minden Pictures).
Cover photograph of a herd of European bison reproduced with permission of istockphoto (© Linda More).

We would like to thank Michael Bright for his invaluable help in the preparation of this book.

Contents

Some words are shown in bold, **like this.** You can find out what they mean by looking in the glossary.

Where is Europe?

We divide the world into seven large areas of land called **continents**. Europe is the second-smallest continent. Europe has a large area of mainland and many islands, such as the United Kingdom.

NORTH AMERICA

EUROPE

ASIA

ATLANTIC OCEAN

AFRICA

PACIFIC OCEAN

PACIFIC OCEAN

SOUTH AMERICA

INDIAN OCEAN

AUSTRALIA

N

W E

S

ANTARCTICA

Can you see the continent of Europe?

There are many types of **habitat** in Europe. There are long rivers, high mountains, rolling hills, leafy woodlands, and areas of open **plains**. There is also a large area of coastline.

Many animals live in Europe's different habitats.

Animals of Europe

Some animals in Europe are **endangered**. This means there are very few of that type of animal left. If they all die, that type of animal will be **extinct**. An animal that is extinct is gone from the planet forever.

The red squirrel is endangered in the United Kingdom and could be extinct in less than 10 years.

Different types of animals look and behave differently from each other. We sort them into groups to help tell them apart.

Animal classification chart

Amphibian	• lives on land and in water • has damp, smooth skin • has **webbed** feet • lays many eggs	
Bird	• has feathers and wings • hatches out of hard-shelled eggs	
Fish	• lives in water • has **fins** and most have **scales** • young hatch from soft eggs	
Mammal	• drinks milk when a baby • has hair on its body	
Reptile	• has scales on its body • lives on land • young hatch from soft-shelled eggs	

Look out for pictures like these next to each photo. They will tell you what type of animal each photo shows.

The United Kingdom

Some of the United Kingdom's **endangered** animals live in woodlands and **wetlands**. Wetlands are areas of shallow water by trees. People destroy these **habitats** for wood, for farmland, and to build on.

This map shows some of the United Kingdom's wild places.

ORKNEYS

HEBRIDES

wetlands

NORTHWEST HIGHLANDS

ATLANTIC OCEAN

GRAMPIAN MOUNTAINS

NORTH SEA

NORTHERN IRELAND

SOUTHERN UPLANDS

River Tweed

wetlands

Wetlands

woodlands

ISLE OF MAN

Lake District

PENNINES

IRELAND

CAMBRIAN MOUNTAINS

River Severn

River Trent

woodlands

woodlands

River Thames

woodlands

N
W E
S

Dormice need trees to survive. They sleep in trees during the day and feed in trees at night. In autumn, they fill up on fruit, nuts, and **insects**, and sleep all winter in nests made of **bark** and grass.

Dormice spend up to three-quarters of their life asleep!

Scottish wild cats live in woodlands. During the day, they rest in trees, old fox dens, and on rocks. They hunt for rabbits or young deer at dawn and dusk. Females have up to eight kittens every year!

Wild cat kittens can hiss and spit at things that upset them after they are a week old!

A bittern's brown feathers help it to hide from **predators** in muddy wetlands.

Bitterns need wetlands to survive. They hunt for fish in the shallow water. Males make loud booming noises to attract females to lay eggs here. They can be heard from several kilometres away!

Western Europe

Some **endangered** animals in western Europe live on islands around the long coastline, in mountains, or in woodlands.

Part of western Europe is a peninsula, which is a long area of land surrounded by water.

ATLANTIC OCEAN

Loire River

AZORES

MADEIRA

CANARY ISLANDS

CANTABRIAN MOUNTAINS

woodlands

Duoro River

PYRENEES MOUNTAINS

Garonne R.

woodlands

Tagus River

woodlands

N
W E
S

The Azorean bat rests in trees, buildings, and caves on the Azores islands at night. It is one of the only bats that hunt for **insects** during the day. **Predators** do not try to catch it during the day!

The Azorean bat is endangered because people disturb its **roosts** and cut down trees.

The Montseny brook newt lives in cold, fast-flowing mountain streams. Its skin has poisons that stop predators from eating it. Its **habitats** are drying up because people take the water to sell in bottles.

This newt's bright colours warn predators that it has poisonous skin.

This lynx climbs and swims well and travels far each day in search of food.

The Iberian lynx uses its sharp eyesight and huge, tufted ears to locate **prey**. It mainly eats rabbits, usually one a day. When people clear its forest habitat for farmland, it has fewer rabbits to eat.

15

Central and northern Europe

Some **endangered** animals in central and northern Europe live in woodlands and rivers. People destroy animal homes when they cut down trees, and they disturb animals by building **dams** on rivers.

This map shows central and northern Europe.

N
W · E
S

NORWEGIAN
SEA

KJOLEN MOUNTAINS

woodlands

woodlands

River Elbe

River

River Dnieper

CARPATHIAN
MOUNTAINS

woodlands

BLACK SEA

ALPS

River Danube

The European bison is the biggest, heaviest mammal in Europe, but it can still jump over streams and run fast! It needs woodlands to survive because it eats leaves, trees, **bark**, and berries from trees.

Bison are as tall as a man and live in groups called **herds**.

In rivers, young eels feed on small animals at night and rest in mud during the day.

Young European eels hatch from eggs in the ocean and drift into rivers, where they feed and grow. Later, adults swim to the ocean, have young, and die. Some get trapped in dams on their journey.

The Danube salmon is a fierce fish! It catches all kinds of river animals in its mouth, which is full of sharp, cone-shaped teeth. Dams stop it from swimming to areas in which it usually lays eggs.

This huge salmon can grow to 1.8 metres (6 feet) in length — as long as a man!

Southern Europe

Southern Europe is a warm, sunny area. People disturb some animals here by visiting or building on the coast or on the inland **wetlands**. People also harm animals by dropping rubbish in the sea.

woodlands
woodlands
woodlands
woodlands
BLACK SEA
Po River
River Danube
wetlands
APENNINES
CORSICA
BALEARIC ISLANDS
SARDINIA
SICILY
MEDITERRANEAN SEA
CRETE
CYPRUS
N
W E
S

This map shows southern Europe.

The slender-billed curlew pulls **prey** from the mud with its long, curved beak.

The slender-billed curlew wades slowly through wetlands. It pecks at the mud to find worms, **insects**, and shellfish to eat. People hunted it for food and are now taking over its wetland **habitats**, too.

The Mediterranean monk seal feeds on fish and octopus. Then it comes onto beaches to rest. People take over the beaches, so it has nowhere to rest. Fishermen also kill the seal to stop it from eating fish.

These seals are some of the most **endangered** mammals in the world.

Some sea turtles get hit by boats when they swim to the surface to breathe.

The loggerhead turtle's strong **jaws** crush shellfish, crabs, and jellyfish. Sadly, some turtles die when they mistake floating plastic bags for jellyfish. Some drown when they get tangled in fishing nets.

Eastern Europe

In eastern Europe, there are mountains, rivers, and open **plains** with areas of **wetlands.** People take over plains and **drain** wetlands for farming. They catch animals for food and **pollute** rivers, too.

There are many mountains in eastern Europe.

grasslands

grasslands

grasslands

CARPATHIAN MOUNTAINS

River Danube

wetlands

SEA OF AZOV

CAUCASUS

TRANSYLVANIAN ALPS

BLACK SEA

BALKAN MOUNTAINS

N
W E
S

MEDITERRANEAN SEA

The sociable lapwing feeds and nests on open land. It walks along, picking up **insects** to eat. It lays eggs in dips in the soil. People take the land the sociable lapwing lives on for farming, and farm animals trample lapwing nests.

At 5 metres (16 feet) long, the beluga sturgeon is the biggest fish in Europe's rivers. It swims into rivers to lay its eggs on rocks. People take these eggs to sell as an expensive food called caviar.

The barbels in front of the sturgeon's mouth feel for fish and other **prey** on the riverbed.

The desman uses its **webbed** feet to paddle along and its long nose as a snorkel!

The Russian desman eats fish, insects, and other prey, but it is at risk from habitat loss. It is also eaten by animals such as mink, which people put in rivers to catch for their fur.

Helping Europe's animals

Some countries in Europe protect animals in **reserves**. These are places where animals can live safely. Hunting nearly made the Alpine ibex **extinct**, but now it lives safely in the Alps.

The Alpine ibex is a wild goat that lives in the mountains of the Alps.

You can help **endangered** animals, too! Try not to disturb animals when you are walking in nature, and don't drop litter. Animals can get trapped in it or harmed when they swallow it.

Why not help animals by helping at a local litter clean-up?

Glossary

bark outer covering of a tree

continent one of seven large areas that make up the world's land

dam barrier that holds back water on a river

drain to cause water to leave something, like a pond

endangered when a type of animal is in danger of dying out

extinct no longer alive; not seen in the wild for 50 years

fin flat body part that sticks out of a fish's body and helps it steer and move

habitat place where plants and animals live

herd group of animals

insect small animal with six legs, such as an ant or fly

jaws part of an animal's body that contains its mouth and teeth

plain large area of flat land with few trees

pollute to poison or damage air, water, or land

predator animal that catches and eats other animals for food

prey animal that gets caught and eaten by other animals

reserve large area of land where plants and animals are protected

roost place where bats and birds sleep or rest

scale small, overlapping pieces that cover an animal's body

webbed when feet have skin between the toes

wetland land covered in shallow water

Find out more

Books

Endangered Animals (Trailblazers), David Orme (Ransom Publishing, 2009)

Europe's Most Amazing Animals (Animal Top Tens), Anita Ganeri (Raintree, 2008)

Internet sites

gowild.wwf.org.uk

Go Wild is the children's club of WWF. You can learn about different animals and their habitats.

www.oum.ox.ac.uk/thezone/animals/extinct/index.htm

Find out about some animals that are now extinct on this website.

Index